YOGA IN THE CLASSROOM
A step-by-step manual for K-12 school teachers

For Deb

And all the great conversation
to come.

Love,

Gail

Yoga
in the
CLASSROOM

A Step-By-Step Manual for K-12 School Teachers

Gail Bentley Walsh

Yoga Mountain Press

132 PARK AVE, NEW CITY, NY 10956

ISBN 10: 0-9817955-0-1
ISBN 13: 978-0-9817955-0-8

Published by
Yoga Mountain Press

Editors: Lynn Milstein and Janet Vignola
Graphic Design and Layout: Holly Seeger

ACKNOWLEDGEMENTS

This book is dedicated to my mother, Margaret Cannon Bentley, whose sweetness and earthly southern grounding rooted me deep in the soil, and to my father, J. Marvin Bentley, whose idealistic mind and spirit found nothing to be impossible.

I thank Lynn Milstein for giving me the encouragement and constant advice and guidance to stay the course and make this book a reality. I thank Janet Vignola for her quick and thorough editing and suggestions, Stephanie Sirico for all her technical and expert computer help, and Holly Seeger for her artistic vision in bringing the book through to completion. I thank my friend, the painter, Leigh Anne Eagerton, for making the brush illustrations happen by giving me the tools and the confidence to go there.

Gratitude to my yoga teachers, especially Paula Heitzner.

I thank my husband, the sculptor Edward J. Walsh, for standing by me with food, funny faces, and love.

Contents

A Special Note to the Teacher

This book is built on the practice of yoga as a gentle exploration; postures and breathing are never forced. If any discomfort is felt, the student is reminded to simply take a breath and slowly come out of the posture. Most of us experience occasional aches and pains when doing any form of exercise. All the postures and breathing techniques described in this book may be simplified and adapted for individuals or groups of students living with limitations.

Individual considerations may be necessary in the classroom. Students with medical health issues or conditions may need a doctor's permission to participate in yoga. Students with particular health concerns such as, for example, a back injury, diabetes, abnormal blood pressure, epilepsy, should definitely have their doctor's permission before practicing yoga.

This or any other exercise program may result in injury.

The author and publisher of this book disclaim any liability arising from any loss, injury, or damage that may result from the use, proper or improper, of any exercise or advice contained in this book.

Introduction

This manual is a guide for exploring yoga along with your students in the classroom. You can use it whether you have never practiced yoga, or you are an experienced practitioner. It will give you, as educators, a tool to help students reduce their stress, increase their concentration, and improve their inner abilities to keep flexible mentally and strong physically.

The unique thing about the **Yoga Mountain** approach to using yoga in the classroom is our emphasis on the teacher as well as the student. Through studying these postures, breathing techniques, meditations and visualizations with your students, you will receive countless benefits. You don't have to actually do the poses; you can simply use the stick figure illustrations and step-by-step instructions.

Teachers that use **Yoga Mountain Yoga in the Classroom©** say these practices – a round of Complete Yoga Breaths, for example, or a full posture workout at the desk, go so far to settle, invigorate, and focus their students that they actually gain class time (and a lot more patience) through the process.

Recent brain research demonstrates how learning stops the instant the "fight or flight response" kicks in. In normal life, the entire autonomic nervous system undergoes regular states of settling and activity. In many of our lives today, however, we miss the "settling," bear down constantly and aggressively on the "activity," and get stuck in the "fight or flight" mode. Yoga gives us simple breathing, stretching, and mindfulness tools to free us from this self-depleting cycle.

One thing certain about all of us is that we are constantly changing. Development never ceases. Learning is always taking place and, as educators, we know that learning is the munificent key to life.

The word yoga means union; it is a three thousand-year-old practice that joins the mind and body through breath. In the **Yoga Mountain Yoga in the Classroom©** program, it also joins the teacher with the student in an open-minded quest for health and harmony.

Teaching Methodology

Yoga is inherently a method of instruction. Doing the breathing and mindfulness together, and trying out the stretches, teaches us essential things about ourselves. First and most important, it teaches self-awareness and self-regulation. Practitioners consciously register how they feel, and are encouraged to breathe through their feelings. They then see themselves in a different light, with some degree of detachment. That's why it's said, "Yoga practice brings freedom." We begin to be more than subjects of our passing emotions, attitudes and fears. How can this make us better learners? Because we are not gripped by anxiety, we've learned not escape (flight) or refusal (fight), but patience and self-regulation. Self-regulation, as defined by the Oxford English Dictionary (1993) is "regulation, control, or direction of one by oneself; regulation from within or without intervention."

Yoga teaches us to trust ourselves.

Yoga postures are not something to be achieved, but a means of self-exploration. A stretch is a question – where to now? A conscious full breath is an inquiry: the mind follows the awareness, which travels inward along with the breath. Mindfulness, meditation, visualization, repetition of a mantra or sound, deep relaxation – these techniques give us mental space to wonder and muse and inquire. They teach us that we are not confined and defined by how our bodies appear.

Socrates, the Greek philosopher, proposed we acknowledge that we already know what we need to know. This is the doctrine of recollection. And here the ancient Greek philosophy is startlingly similar to the yoga philosophy that wisdom lies within each and every one of us.

The secret to learning yoga as you teach it is being humble. You put yourself in a place where you're not the expert who already knows the facts; you're not the judge who will decide whether or not your students get it right – you are learning simultaneously with them.

The Science of Yoga

The story of the "relaxation response" and the "fight or flight response" is a story of scientific discovery. In 1915, Dr. Walter Cannon first used the nomen "fight or flight response" – a genetic wisdom (so he said) hard wired into our brains to keep us from harm.

Dr. Walter Cannon was a physiologist at Harvard, and his studies describe the release of chemicals adrenaline, noradrenaline and cortisol into the blood stream, and the patterns of nerve cell firing in the hypothalamus at the center front of the brain, when something startles or scares us. Blood pressure, heart rate, and breathing rate all increase markedly. The elicitation of the "fight or flight response" also depresses the immune system.

Years later, in 1975, Dr. Herbert Benson published his groundbreaking book, *The Relaxation Response*. The "relaxation response" is the opposite of the "fight or flight response." It is associated with decreased metabolism, blood pressure, heart rate, breathing rate, and stabilization of blood-flow to the muscles. Skin resistance increases, and more alpha, theta, and delta waves are produced in the brain. Herbert Benson, M.D., is the Director Emeritus of the Benson-Henry Institute (BHI), and Mind/Body Medical Institute Associate Professor of Medicine, Harvard Medical School.

In his studies, Dr. Benson found that practicing meditation along with yoga stretches proved beneficial for the health of the heart. He emphasizes that a wide variety of relaxation techniques can elicit the same set of physiologic changes. If students run or play ball they'll likely have the same "relaxation response." But it's not possible in our schools to have constant outdoor physical activity.

These are not yes or no, black or white conditions, but full of gradations in intensity. The "fight or flight" is the state we're in when we are in the real or imagined presence of danger; the "relaxation response" is the state we are in when we are in the real or imagined presence of ease.

Yoga practice doesn't suppress or block emotions and memories and impulses, but encourages us to see where they commence and how they take us over. That's why yoga is called a science of the mind. The science is internal, a personal science. By observing, knowing, and accepting ourselves more openly, the feelings flow more freely.

The *New Shorter Oxford English Dictionary (1993 Edition)* defines "science" as the state or fact of knowing. As they say in the school of life – "You know what you know."

If we don't intervene on our own behalf when we're feeling stressed, who will?

The following quote is from another Harvard professor, the great medical author and MD (Medical Doctor), Thomas Lewis.

"We are paying too little attention, and respect, to the built-in durability and sheer power of the human organism. Its surest tendency is toward stability and balance. It is a distortion, with something profoundly disloyal about it, to picture the human being as a teetering, fallible contraption, always needing watching and patching, always on the verge of flapping to pieces; this is the doctrine that people hear most often, and most eloquently, on all our information media."

- Thomas Lewis, *Lives of a Cell,* p. 83, Penguin Books, 1978

Grades K-12
The Main Meditation Poses

The traditional yoga poses for meditation and mindfulness are especially loved by children. Practitioners of all ages focus on these poses, as they align the spine and tone and stretch the muscle systems that support it. The poses are 100% the same; but the names vary according to the age group.

Child's Pose
is called **Child's Pose** by children
and grown ups alike.

Zazen,
Japanese Sitting Pose
called *Vajrasana* (Diamond [adamantine] in Sanskrit)
by adult yogis, and *Squirrel* by children.

Easy Seated Cross-Legged Pose
is what children call
Kris-Cross-Applesauce or *The Pretzel*

Float Pose
(*Shavasana* in Sanskrit)
is called *Corpse* by adults.

We "grow" gradually into the ability to do these *Main Meditation Poses* with ease. Save the study of them until you go through the *Everyday Lessons*. Never force these postures. If it's difficult at first to drop the hips back and sit on the heels in *Zazen*, for instance, use a pillow or rolled yoga mat between hips and heels, or a pillow under the feet.

Grades K-12
Interactive Story and Learning Context

Three ways to learn: watching/observing; sounding/speaking; moving/acting.

*The other day I woke up in the **Child's Pose** and heard drums beating down in the woods. I sat up right away in the **Squirrel Pose** and listened. The drums got louder. I dropped to the **Dog Pose** and sniffed the air. I was ready to run but I needed a good stretch first, so I yawned and stretched in the **Downward Dog** and then in the **Upward Dog**.*

*The drums came closer. I felt a little scared and arched up into the **Cat Pose**. Then I did the **Lion** - I roared three times, loud and strong.*

*The drums were silent. Maybe I scared them away. I sat back in the **Squirrel Pose** again to listen. Then I quickly slithered down into the **Snake Pose (Cobra)**, so I could hide in the grass and see what was going on. I saw a boy and a girl coming out of the woods. They were playing flutes and leading a parade of animals - an eagle, an elephant, a lion and a turtle. The animals were humming and slapping their feet on the ground and clapping their hands, and that was what was making the drumming sound. They came up to me and circled around me and I started humming – humm, jumped up, slapped my feet on the ground, went into **Hanuman's Lunge**, and marched off with them back into the woods.*

The above yoga story was made up by a group of six-year-olds. Some of the animals are well-known yoga postures, but the turtle and the elephant were created on the spot. Students in kindergarten through the second and third grades like to choose their own postures and string them together in sequences and stories. They also like to make up original postures.

Fourth and fifth graders enjoy activities such as moving person to person in a circle with each person leading a posture, and creating storyboards (live or on paper) of yoga adventures.

Seventh, eighth and ninth grade girls enjoy keeping yoga journals about their experience, and round-table discussions about what they learn. The boys like Relay Vinyasa where one group goes and then the next. Boys also enjoy Googling athletes who do yoga and bringing in their stories to tell the class.

High school students might begin to think of themselves as yoga warriors – out to save the world by becoming self-disciplined and mindful. Diaries and journals are important for them, and projected stories of what lies in their personal future. A journal can be a living narrative – it doesn't have to be written down.

Meditation and Breathing Techniques

The following seven yoga techniques elicit the "relaxation response." They refer us back to our internal experience and awareness. In the ***Everyday Yoga Lessons Standing - A*** part of this manual, you will find these techniques interspersed along with the postures. They are appropriate for K-12 and with every student population.

*Focus on the **Complete Yoga Breath** to start, and keep using it with your students until you feel confident and relaxed about doing it any time. Then move on gradually, one by one, to the other techniques, making sure you come back often to the **Complete Yoga Breath**.*

The Complete Yoga Breath – Diaphragmatic Breathing

The ***Complete Yoga Breath*** is exactly that: complete. For young children we sometimes get them to lie on the back with a teddy on the belly and make (watch) that teddy rise and fall. With older students, the idea is to fill completely - the belly, solar plexus, diaphragm, upper chest, even the back like a balloon, and then deflate and let the breath go. Interestingly, most of us cut short the exhale rather than the inhale. It seems we're in such a hurry. So what happens is that the next inhale is shallow, because we haven't emptied the lungs completely. Sometimes we say to students, inhale and let that ***Complete Yoga Breath*** saturate every cell, every part of you, with insight and energy and courage. Now let that exhale be nice and long, twice as long as the inhale, and let that exhale take with it everything you don't need. This breath can be done over and over while doing a yoga posture, or all alone as a meditation and/or relaxation technique.

The Sounding Breath

The **Sounding Breath**, known as **Ujjayi** *(victorious)* **Breath** in Sanskrit, is said to be the most balancing and calming breathing technique in yoga because of its stimulating and massaging affect on the thyroid gland in the throat, the echo in the nasal passages and sinuses and ear drums, and the release of tension in the jaw, throat, shoulders, mouth and tongue. In the **Sounding Breath**, we breathe with the lips gently closed, the epiglottis slightly constricted, so the breath sounds like the waves in the ocean (or Darth Veda). Another way to teach this is to blow in the palm of the hand like you want to make your breath condense on a windowpane. Then do the same, minus the hand, but with the mouth softly closed. This breath (like all yoga breaths) can be done over and over while doing a yoga posture or all alone, as a meditation/relaxation.

Breath of Fire

The **Breath of Fire**, also known as **Bastriki Breath**, is the most energizing breath in yoga. It gets the blood pumping and the whole body flushed with fresh oxygen, particularly the brain (which uses up most of the body's oxygen in the first place). For children we call this the **Bunny Breath**. It's a light, panting breath, and shouldn't be done forcefully. The Lamaze method of breath technique for birthing got its origin here. This breath is said to bring fresh insight and knowledge and courage, because it oxygenates the brain. Try it only 10 rounds (breaths) or so at first; and then perhaps build up to 20 rounds (inhales and exhales). Stop between rounds and breathe normally for thirty seconds or more before trying the **Breath of Fire** again. Three rounds of 20 breaths each is your base-line target. Like all yoga breaths, it can be done standing or seated. It might be good to try it seated initially as some students may feel light-headed when they first try it. If someone does feel light-headed, they should stop and rest. Remember – it's a light, panting breath. Do not make it forceful!

Progressive Muscle Relaxation

Progressive Muscle Relaxation, described by Edmund Jacobson in the early 1920's, is a method of reducing anxiety and tension by learning to relax the muscles. Have the students sitting at their desks, or lying prone or supine if possible on the floor. Take them in a quiet voice, step by step, through the body.

- *Tense the toes, squeeze, contract them together, pull them apart and tense.*
- *Relax the toes and let go any tension there.*
- *Tense the feet, squeeze, contract them tense, relax the feet and let go any tension there.*
- *Tense the ankles, squeeze, contract them tense, relax the ankles and let go any tension there.*
- *Tense the lower legs, squeeze, contract them tense, relax the lower legs and let go any tension there.*
- *And so on through the body — knees, thighs, hips, waist, rib cage, chest, hands, lower arms, upper arms, neck, face muscles, scalp, and brain.*

You may vary the progression, changing the focus to one part of the body.

For example, the shoulders;
    – lift and tighten the scapula,
    – release;
    – tighten the base of the neck,
    – release; etc.

Even only a minute is good if that's all the time you have!

Visualization

Visualizations take your students on journeys of the imagination by the simplest discreet yet concrete suggestions. Keys to the art of guided visualization are economy, precision of words and timing; get students to be specific about details the mind perceives - the smells, sights and sounds. Music can be a soothing accompaniment to the journey; but it's not a necessity. Have students do a few stretches first, then sit with heads down on the desks or lie down.

Here are two guided Visualization scripts, excellent for all ages, which you may read out loud to your students:

A Healing and Cleansing Visualization

Visualize the breath flowing in on the inhale, blue and green, like water, filling every cell in your body with healing energy; see the breath saturating the cells, penetrating deeply and washing over every atom.

Visualize the breath on the exhale now, taking with it all the disease, anger, hurt and frustration, emptying out all your confusion, pain and stiffness.

A Peaceful Place Visualization

Close your eyes, breathe, and imagine you are on a path to a place no one knows but you. It's grassy and soft on your feet, on a warm, sunny day with a light breeze touching your cheeks and forehead . . . you can feel that soft breeze.

There's an entrance up ahead that leads to your secret place. It may be made of bushes or clouds or trees or covered with sparkles like a fantasy door – whatever your imagination offers – Picture that entrance and make it your own. Give it a texture, a color; see its shape, its size, and make it a clear image in your mind's eye.

You arrive at that entrance and open it and step inside. Your peaceful place is there for you, all around you, however you imagine it – it may be a sandy beach by the sea, a shady patch in the deep woods – whatever place you want it to be, and you lie down there and stretch out and rest. Your breath is deep and slow and feels good and there's nothing you have to do.

[Note: Allow some silent time here, three to fifteen minutes or more, according to your class schedule.]

Gradually begin to wake and come back. Draw in air, rise, and walk back through the door, closing it behind you; keeping your secret place inside you. You can go back there any time you wish.

Breath or Mantra Meditation

1. Choose a short phrase or a word that holds great meaning for you.

2. Sit down on a chair in a quiet environment.

3. Close your eyes.

4. Use three deep breaths to completely relax the body.

5. Breathe slowly and naturally. As you do, focus on your word or phrase. Repeat it to yourself each time you exhale. If your thoughts distract you, simply return to repeating your word or phrase.

6. Continue the technique for ten to twenty minutes. Use this technique upon waking in the morning, or at the same time every day.

Third Eye Visualization/Meditation

Close your eyes and imagine there is a line inside your head from the bridge of your nose to the base of your skull. Now imagine another line drawn across your skull about two centimeters in from the eyes. "A small paired cluster of cells in the frontal part of the hypothalamus, 20,000 or so cells known as the suprachiasmatic nuclei (SCN), identified by scientists as the 'mind's clock,' is at the intersection of these imaginary lines."[1]

Focus inwardly on the spot where they intersect. You can focus by breathing in and out slowly from the "third eye."

Yogis name this spot the "third eye" as it is supposed to open in enlightenment. They believe that if you focus on this spot and empty yourself of all other thoughts, this inward contemplation centers and calms one.

---

1 *Rhythms of Life*; p. 67, Yale University Press 2004; Russell G. Foster & Leon Kreitzman

Everyday Yoga Lessons Standing - A

Hanuman's Reach
(A-1)

Slump / Hunch
(A-2)

Farmer's Pose
(A-3)

Willow
(A-4)

Spinal Twist Spiral
(A-5)

Lion
(A-11)

King/Queen Dancer
(A-12)

Tree Pose
(A-13)

Cow's Arch
(A-14)

Forward Bend
(A-15)

Half-Moon Pose
(A-21)

Side-Leg Lift
(A-22)

Revolved
Side-Angle Pose
(A-23)

Revolved Triangle
(A-24)

Tortoise
(A-25)

Everyday Yoga Lessons Standing - A

Mountain Pose
(A-6)

Wide-Leg Forward
Bend w/ Yoga Mudra
(A-7)

Standing
Knee-to-Chest
(A-8)

Standing Stick
(A-9)

Proud Warrior
(A-10)

Still Dancer
(A-16)

Warrior One
(A-17)

Triangle Pose
(A-18)

Hanuman's Lunge
(A-19)

Extended
Side-Angle Pose
(A-20)

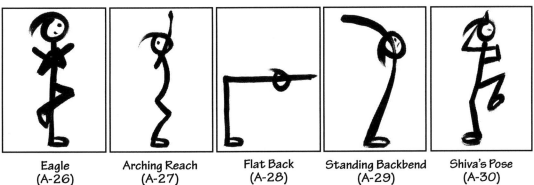

Eagle
(A-26)

Arching Reach
(A-27)

Flat Back
(A-28)

Standing Backbend
(A-29)

Shiva's Pose
(A-30)

How to Use The Everyday Lessons

Everyday Yoga Lessons Standing - A are easy, standing asanas (postures) that may be practiced beside the desk individually or in combinations. In yoga, we generally do each asana more than once. The first pass introduces the pose; the second pass takes us deeper into the experience.

Let's say you have only a few minutes for yoga at the beginning of the school day: you start with the first posture and do it twice. Do not hurry the process. Students (and you) may be impatient at first. Most of us are so accustomed to being incessantly distracted and/or entertained. Remember, we are going for depth of internal experience, and that experience will not be registered by the mind if you push or rush.

When you first work with this manual, we suggest that the initial one to ten *Everyday Yoga Lessons Standing - A* be followed sequentially. Afterwards, feel free to jump around and group any two, three or more together.

Everyday Yoga Lessons Standing - A
— EACH LISTING IN THIS SECTION FOLLOWS THIS FORMAT —

Pose name – the name of the yoga pose or posture.

Inquiry "question" – a simple, optional question to get everyone thinking.

Description – a basic overview of the posture.

Instruction – how to do the posture.

Breath & Meditation – suggestions for incorporating breath and mindfulness.

Anecdote – myths and tales about the posture.

Anatomy & Physiology – tips for understanding how the pose might affect the body and mind.

Hanuman's Reach (A-1)

What does it mean to stretch, to go beyond the old place?

Description

This posture is a great energizer – a metaphor for yearning that gives a sense of exhilaration. Did you ever feel you wanted to bust out of your skin – well this posture allows you to try and do just that.

Instruction

Reach your arms up as high as you can and go on tiptoe and put everything you have into it. Try looking up.

Breath & Meditation

Breathe in deeply through the nasal passages; breathe out through the mouth or nose. Take three ***Complete Yoga Breaths*** (a breath is an inhale and an exhale) if possible when you're high up in the posture. The meditation here is in the awareness of the breath.

Anecdote

Hanuman in Sanskrit is "monkey," but this monkey is said to have the energy to scramble all over the world. Her/His potential for unbridled curiosity and movement is endless.

Anatomy & Physiology

Stretches every muscle in the body, stimulates the circulation and metabolism, and energizes the brain by bringing in more oxygen.

Slump / Hunch (A-2)

What does it mean to be free of tension, totally at ease?

Description

This posture is a deep release of tension – a metaphor for letting go that gives a sense of complete relaxation. Did you ever feel you wanted to give up, just for a while, the struggle to get everything right? This asana encourages you to just hang loose completely and let the whole creature that you are calm down.

Instruction

Stand with the feet parallel, knees relaxed over the feet, and let the chin drop toward the chest and the head hang. Now let the shoulders and upper back round over, letting go all tension and all effort, so you're looking down toward your knees.

Breath & Meditation

Breathe in through the nasal passages; breathe out through the mouth or nose. Take three long gentle inhales and exhales while you're slumped in the posture. The meditation here is in the awareness of the breath.

Anecdote

This is a homemade asana; you won't find it in the yoga books.

Anatomy & Physiology

The ***Slump/Hunch*** allows the solar plexus area - encompassing the stomach, pancreas, liver, gallbladder, small intestine (duodenum) and kidneys - to release and relax completely. In yoga, they say we armor ourselves and store fear in this area. The "flight or fight response" starts here: we grip in reaction to real or perceived danger. This posture puts us in touch with quieting that anxiety and fear.

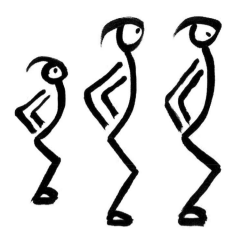

Farmer's Pose (A-3)

What does it mean to arch the spine? What part of the spine is actually arching?

Description

This posture is a dramatic opener of the lungs and entire ribcage. In the dance world and in physical therapy this arched position is called extension (as opposed to flexion when the spine bends forward). Notice how the shoulder blades (called scapulae) draw down and toward each other in the back.

Instruction

Stand with the feet parallel, hip-width apart. Bring the hands behind with the elbows bent to press the palms against the lower back (sacrum area). Lift the head and look up as you press against the sacrum and lift the chest.

Breath & Meditation

Breathe in through the nasal passages; breathe out through the mouth or nose. Take three breaths if possible when you're arched up in the posture. The meditation here is in the awareness of the breath.

Anecdote

This is called the **Farmer's Pose** because picking the crop was backbreaking work. After leaning over and picking beans or cotton or whatever, farmers would straighten up and bring their hands to the back and stretch in an extension. It relieves sore back.

Anatomy & Physiology

Brings more oxygen to the lungs, stretches the muscles of the chest and upper back; also patterns the shoulders to release and drop down.

Willow (A-4)

What does it mean to "go with the flow?"

Description

This posture is a leaning out to one side, then the other side, in a stretch that massages all the internal organs of the abdomen. It's called a lateral move - side to side.

Instruction

Stand with the feet hip-width apart and parallel, knees relaxed. Stretch the arms overhead with palms facing each other. Give yourself space between your hands, so your shoulders can drop and be free, and you can soften around your shoulder sockets. (Where are the shoulder sockets anyway? A close look anatomically with a skeletal poster is suggested.) Now simply stretch up and to the right, take a few breaths there, and back to the left.

Breath & Meditation

Breathe in deeply through the nasal passages; breathe out through the mouth or nose. Breathe in as you stretch to one side, breathe out as you come back to center; breathe in as you stretch to the other side, breathe out as you come back to center. The meditation here is in the awareness of the breath.

Anecdote

Whoever has the wisdom to bend will not break under stress.

Anatomy & Physiology

The *Willow* tones and stretches and strengthens the core abdominal muscles.

Spinal Twist Spiral (A-5)

What is the basic movement pattern of life on earth?
What is DNA and what does it look like?

Description

This posture wrings out the insides, stimulating the internal organs, stirring things up by pushing and pulling. The spongy disks (What are spongy disks of the vertebrae?) of the spinal vertebrae are rocked and rolled and coo like a baby.

Instruction

Stand with the feet hip-width apart, feet parallel, knees relaxed. Look around to your left, follow the movement with the shoulders, continue with the entire chest, have the arms follow the movement with elbows bent and hands toward the hips. The position of the head is important in that you want openness at the base of the skull. Drop the chin slightly to open the base of the skull. Come back to center and reverse on the other side.

Breath & Meditation

Breathe in through the nasal passages; breathe out through the mouth or nose. Inhale and turn, exhale and relax and hold the turn; inhale and turn further, exhale and relax and release. Repeat on the other side. The meditation here is in the awareness of the breath.

Anecdote

The first yogi was said to be a fish, *Matsyendra (Lord of Fish)* in Sanskrit. *Matsyendra* is also Sanskrit for the spinal twist.

Anatomy & Physiology

The spinal twist fans the gastric fire (gets things moving), stimulating and cleansing the liver, massages all the internal organs and is said to help cure "all diseases." It awakens the dormant energy within.

Mountain Pose (A-6)

What does it mean to be centered?
Is there an actual center to each of us?

Description

This is a deep centering posture.

Instruction

Stand with the feet hip-width apart and close your eyes, imagining the mountain shape. As a variation, the mountain may be done with arms up, clasping (or not) the hands overhead. When you breathe into the belly, the belly expands; as you breathe out and draw the muscles of the lower belly inward toward the lower back (on the exhale), you become aware of your center (the core muscles of the abdominal area) and how your center is strong.

Breath & Meditation

Here we continue our study of the ***Complete Yoga Breath (Diaphragmatic Breathing)*** or, as some call it, Three-Part Breathing. Draw the breath deep into the belly, then the rib cage, then the upper chest. Exhale the upper chest, rib cage, and belly. Do this in the asana counting slowly in and out. Keep your attention focused on the sensations of the breath. The meditation here is in awareness of the three-part breaths.

Anecdote

The ***Mountain Pose*** makes us more conscious of where we are now – perhaps restless and angry, and where we might be someday through the practice of yoga – more calm and self-composed.

Anatomy & Physiology

The ***Mountain Pose*** grounds us; we feel rooted in the earth.

Wide-Leg Forward Bend with Yoga Mudra (A-7)

What is the meaning of yielding?
Letting go?

Description
This is a deep yielding posture.

Instruction
Stand in a wide-leg position with feet parallel and knees relaxed. Clasp the hands behind the back with the palms facing each other. Stretch the arms and hands back so the wings (shoulder blades, scapulae) are drawn closer together. Relax the knees and begin to hang over forward letting the head hang down between the legs, along with the entire torso. When the torso hangs over from the hip sockets and the knees are relaxed, enjoy it and breathe deeply. Come out slowly with knees relaxed and let the head come up last.

Breath & Meditation
Take three ***Complete Yoga Breaths*** and let go totally while inverted. These numbers may be increased to nine breaths, twelve breaths.

Anecdote
In yoga a *mudra* is a physical seal. The *mudra* here refers to hands clasped behind with palms facing each other.

Anatomy & Physiology
Forward bends stretch all the muscles through the legs and back, including the neck, and bring more oxygen to the brain. They relieve stress dramatically and increase alertness and concentration. Adding the ***Yoga Mudra*** here opens the upper chest, expands the collarbone, stretches and tones the muscles surrounding the shoulders and upper arms.

Standing Knee-to-Chest (A-8)

What is core strength? Where is core strength?
Do we come with it or is it developed by us?

Description

This is a balancing pose, focusing on a point ahead, engaging core strength to hold you upright on one foot.

Instruction

Stand with feet parallel, breathe deeply. Put all your weight on the right foot and engage your core strength by drawing the muscles of the lower belly inward toward the sacrum in the lower back. Bring the left knee up toward the chest. Hold the bent leg with both hands, drawing the thigh into the belly, shoulders relaxed, and try and count three breaths keeping your balance by standing on one leg. Reverse on the other side.

Breath & Meditation

Three ***Complete Yoga Breaths*** on one leg, then on the other leg. Focus on a point ahead. Here the focus, together with the breath, constitutes the meditation.

Anecdote

Some schools of yoga call this the Breathing Sacrum Pose. It certainly opens and relaxes the sacrum and lower back, and makes that whole area feel healthy.

Anatomy & Physiology

Balancing poses are said to increase concentration and confidence. There is some evidence that they help develop right brain left brain coordination. Engaging your core muscles trains you to move from the core, think from the core. This asana relieves lower back pain by opening and stretching and broadening the bones (hipbone, sacrum) and muscles (sciatic, iliopsoas, etc). (A muscle poster is recommended for reference, along with the skeletal poster.) Identify the bones and muscles, including the core muscles of the abdomen.

Standing Stick (A-9)

What is the definition of balance?
What does it mean to be "off your rocker?"

Description

This asana (posture), literally meaning *'seat'* in Sanskrit, is a mentally and physically challenging exercise that has many steps, any one of which is sufficient.

Instruction

Clasp the arms overhead, elbows straight (if do-able). Focus on a specific point on the wall in front of you. Keep that focus. Take a deep breath. On the exhale, step forward with the right foot, lift the left leg and bring the entire torso and left leg up parallel to the floor.

The important exercise here is to keep the core strong, connect the muscles of the belly to the back internally (engage the core muscles), so that the torso and lifted leg are in a straight line. It's best to come up at perhaps a 15-degree angle, or start at a 5-degree angle, keeping the integrity of the line, and practice that until you can go all the way to a parallel line standing straight over one leg. The core muscles here are used as stabilizers.

Breath & Meditation

Three **Complete Yoga Breaths** on one leg, then on the other leg. Focus on a point ahead. Here the focus, together with the breath, constitutes the meditation.

Anecdote

This asana is often used in yoga therapy to test for core strength.

Anatomy & Physiology

Weightbearing on one leg, strengthening the bones of feet, ankles, knees; this posture integrates core muscles and intent.

Proud Warrior (A-10)

What is the relationship between courage and commitment?

Description

This asana is a wide-open position demanding core strength, balance and coordination.

Instruction

Stand wide-legged, strong contact with floor through the feet, strong core, and spread your arms out to the sides. Turn your left foot so the toes face left. You can do this by simply lifting and rotating the ball of the foot, and leaving the heel in place. Let the ball of the right foot likewise rotate inward to point in the same direction. Your hips are facing forward and your toes are facing left. Bend the left knee so the thigh eventually comes parallel to the floor with the knee directly over the left foot. The right leg stays straight and the right heel pushes outward to keep grounded. Look forward and left alternately. Reverse on the other side.

Breath & Meditation

Nine ***Complete Yoga Breaths*** in the position; repeat in the opposite direction. Focus on a point to your right beyond your hand; reverse on the other side. Here the focus, together with the breath, constitutes the meditation.

Anecdote

In yoga, the warrior essence is in the complete commitment to the task at hand, the purity of the line and the integrity of the whole position. No interference of the ego – no concern with showing off your strength or challenging others.

Anatomy & Physiology

This asana calls on all the systems of the body for coordination and control, including the nervous system, sensory system, and endocrine system.

Lion (A-11)

What is the axial skeleton?
Where in the head do we humans usually hold most tension?

Description

This posture releases tension in the jaw, which is part of the appendicular skeleton, draws energy to the throat, tongue, and neck, and makes people laugh.

Instruction

Sit or stand and make fists with your hands and draw all the negative stuff into your chest on an inhale. On the exhale sprawl out your claws and roar and thrust your head forward stretching your mouth open wide and stretching out your tongue. You may also cross your eyes and look at the tip of your nose, or look at your third eye point.

Breath & Meditation

Draw the breath in fiercely on the inhale, and pour the breath out fiercely on the exhale. The exhale is twice as long as the inhale. The idea is to let go and send off everything you don't need. It's a "cleansing" exercise/meditation.

Anecdote

It's possible to do this internally – in imagination, and start over fresh with whatever you have to deal with.

Anatomy & Physiology

Stretches the jaw to prevent or help to heal TMJ (Temporomandibular Joint Disorder). Expels all the stale air and worn-out thought, so fresh energy and ideas may roll in.

King / Queen Dancer (A-12)

What is the original meaning of royal?
How are the axial and appendicular skeletons woven together?

Description

This asana is a balance plus extension that calls on all our resources.

Instruction

Stand in **Mountain Pose**, lift the right foot behind and clasp the foot with the hands. Relax the standing leg so the knee is not locked, and begin to shift or roll the upper body forward over the left leg, which is stationary. The chest opens wide and the entire torso arches in extension. The main mover of the action is in kicking or pushing the right foot back against the pull of the hands. The pose may also be done with one hand holding the foot and the other hand reaching upward. Reverse on the other side.

Breath & Meditation

Here we begin using the **Sounding Breath**. In Sanskrit, this breath is called **Ujjayi Breath** – which has the meaning of victorious. The mouth is loosely closed. The epiglottis in the throat is slightly constricted and the breath is gently forced through. This gives a sound like the waves in the ocean.

Anecdote

This pose may be considered an experience of self-transcendence. Dance in the face of sadness and depression, dance in gratitude to the universe.

Anatomy & Physiology

This asana helps prevent and heal "frozen shoulder" by broadening the upper chest and deeply stretching the shoulders.

Tree Pose (A-13)

Why is it hard to balance and do other things simultaneously?

Description

This posture creates flexibility in the hips.

Instruction

Just as you thought, you stand on one leg, lift the other leg, holding onto the foot, and place the sole of the foot against the other thigh (not against the knee). If you can't bring the foot up as high as the inner thigh, place it gently along the ankle or lower leg. Try the other side.

Breath & Meditation

Use the ***Sounding Breath*** to make victory possible here. It's mind over matter. Concentrate on making it a light, easy experience. Focus on one spot at eye level and keep that focus.

Anecdote

In yoga, they say we store frustration and anger in the hips; this is because our instinct is to destroy the enemy with a kick or run like mad. Originally our legs were our only weapons, our only defense.

Anatomy & Physiology

When we release all the tension in the hip down through the hanging bent-knee leg, we get better overall circulation and the ability to breathe through stress. Using the ***Sounding Breath*** in this asana creates a calming effect throughout. The circulation and heart rate slow, the respiration becomes even and smooth.

Cow's Arch (A-14)

What does "opposing" mean? Do humans have cuds?

Description

This is a posture with two opposing actions.

Instruction

Stand with your feet together, parallel, and tighten your glutes (your whole bottom) by drawing the muscles fast together. Open your thumbs to create a **Lion's Claw** – a half circle, and bring the claw to the ridge of the pelvis with thumbs in back. Keeping your gluts tight to create a powerful base, let your back sway in extension, chin down toward the chest.

Breath & Meditation

Use the **Sounding Breath** or **Complete Yoga Breaths** and observe yourself closely. Focus on release; hold no tension anywhere in the body. Yes, the glutes are tight; but tight isn't tension necessarily, is it?

Anecdote

Cows are exceedingly relaxed, as their main thing in life is to chew. It's the collapse of all the core stuff that gives folks the freedom of the cow.

Anatomy & Physiology

Engaging the buttocks while keeping the upper torso soft teaches us how we can use our energy precisely. It refines the intelligence and grants us a wider range of both psychological and physical movement.

Forward Bend (A-15)

*Why do all the religions of the world use postures
that represent physical surrender?*

Description

Forward Bend is a metaphor for surrender. It's a giving up of everything you can't control. Handing it over, you might say, to the Great Mystery.

Instruction

Stand with feet parallel, a narrow hip-width apart. Relax the knees, hinge at the hip sockets (use the skeletal poster), reach up and then reach out forward, forward, far as you can go, then let the whole torso fall forward toward the ground. There are a myriad of ways to experience this posture, like bringing the palms to the floor on both sides of the feet, clasping the elbows, or straightening the legs by lifting the hip sockets. The important thing is that the neck, jaw and shoulders are not tight, and the lips are slightly parted. Let all of you surrender, including the belly, including the will.

Breath & Meditation

Six to twelve **Complete Yoga Breaths** in the position. Be particularly aware of the increased space between your twenty-four spinal vertebrae.

Anecdote

You can come up so gradually from this position, keeping your knees relaxed and engaging your core muscles, that when the head finally rights itself, you're in a new place entirely. The slower you do all this, the greater the reward.

Anatomy & Physiology

In this position you get a flood of fresh blood and oxygen to the brain. It is said to reverse the aging process and increase the Intelligence Quotient.

Still Dancer (A-16)

Can a dance be still? Does everyone dance before they are born?

Description

This is a variation on ***Queen/King Dancer (A-12)*** that challenges us to be motionless.

Instruction

Stand in ***Mountain Pose***, lift the right foot behind, and clasp it with the right hand. Relax the standing leg so the knee is not locked. Reach the left hand behind and clasp the same right foot. The chest opens wide and the entire torso very gently arches (extension). Come to stillness. Try the other side.

Breath & Meditation

Meditate on your Sixth Energy Center – your "third eye." It's directly over the bridge of your nose, a quarter-inch in from the flesh of your forehead. It is vertical, not horizontal, and corresponds to the pituitary gland (some say the pineal) in front of the hypothalamus in your brain. When distractions enter, keep bringing your focus back to that vortex.

Anecdote

In the yogic tradition, Masters sometimes stand this way for hours.

Anatomy & Physiology

Recent brain research shows how meditating using breath and visual focus can change the energy in the frontal lobes of the brain, bringing clarity where it was perhaps missing.

Warrior One (A-17)

What makes this a warrior pose?

Description

One of the simplest, most powerful warrior asanas, demonstrating steadiness and ease.

Instruction

Stand wide-legged, strong contact with floor through the feet, strong core, and spread your arms out to the sides. Turn your feet and hips and torso to face right, letting the ball of the left foot rotate inward to follow the move; bend the right knee and keep it stable over the right foot. The hands reach overhead. Try looking up, and try looking forward. Reverse to the other side (illustrated).

Breath & Meditation

Use a light, panting ***Bastriki-Bellows Breath (Breath of Fire)*** in the asana and stay with it 30 seconds, 60 seconds, even as long as 90 seconds if the breath doesn't make you feel dizzy. Focus on the center or your consciousness – the so-called "third eye."

Anecdote

The yogic warrior is recognized as full of steadiness and ease, like ***Hanuman***, striding with exhilaration all over the universe.

Anatomy & Physiology

Strengthens the feet, ankles and legs; develops core awareness; increases balance and concentration; while the ***Breath of Fire*** oxygenates the brain.

Triangle Pose (A-18)

Why is the triangle considered a dynamic shape?

Description

This asana moves the body dynamically outward from three points. It works on the principal of dynamic opposition.

Instruction

Stand with feet wider apart than hips (standing wide-leg position). Open the arms wide, feeling dynamic opposition in the chest and upper back. Keep the hips stable, facing forward, but rotate the feet to face right. Turn the right palm upward and reach out to the right as far as you can go, then drop the arm and rest the back of the hand along the inner right leg or down toward the ankle. The left arm simply reaches upward. Your two legs and your hips form a triangular shape. Open, reach, press and lengthen. The right side of your body, right arm, and right leg form another triangular shape. Imagine you are against a flat plane and bring your upper back and head and hips along that plane internally. To come out, breathe in and lift the arms to bring you upright. Reverse on the other side.

Breath & Meditation

Along with the posture, try three **Complete Yoga Breath** sequences, where each beginning, middle, and end of a breath is marked in the awareness and accounted for. This is a meditation technique as well as a breathing exercise.

Anecdote

The triangle is thought to be a dynamic shape representing unending movement.

Anatomy & Physiology

This asana has a reputation in yoga of correcting all structural misalignments and muscle imbalances. It's another one of those postures that's said to heal all ills. It gets the energy flowing throughout, and works with dynamic opposition.

Hanuman's Lunge (A-19)

Where do you go when you dream of going?

Description

This is a racing, charging flat-out position.

Instruction

Start in wide-legged position, feet parallel but considerably wider apart than the hips. Turn the balls of the feet and the torso and hips to face the right. Bend the right knee so the thigh eventually comes parallel to the floor; drop the left knee to rest on the floor. The arms are straight and the hands are on the floor on both sides of the right foot. Lift the left knee and reach back with the heel.

Reverse to the other side (illustrated).

Last stage (new challenge): Keep the leg position and bring arms straight out forward ahead of you.

Reverse to the other side.

Breath & Meditation

Decide where you want to go, give it a visual representation and set it before you in your mind's eye, so you're moving right toward it.

Anecdote

Remember the monkey – *Hanuman*. Now she's/he's racing over the whole earth.

Anatomy & Physiology

This move energizes the circulatory and respiratory systems, warming up the whole body.

Extended Side-Angle Pose (A-20)

What does integrity mean? Can a line in space have integrity?

Description

This asana is a wide-open position demanding core strength, balance and coordination. It is precisely the same stance as **Proud Warrior** to start, and moves on into the position of the extended torso and the arms.

Instruction

Stand wide-legged, strong contact with floor through the feet, strong core, and spread your arms out to the sides. Turn your right foot so the toes face right. You can do this by simply lifting and rotating the ball of the foot and leaving the heel in place. Let the ball of the left foot likewise rotate inward to point in the same direction. Your hips are facing forward and your toes are facing right. Bend the right knee so the thigh eventually comes parallel to the floor with the knee directly over the right foot. The left leg stays straight and the left heel pushes outward to keep grounded. Look forward and right alternately.

Now onward to the Extended Side-Angle Pose (illustrated)!

Reach your right arm and your torso out over your bent knee. Bend the elbow and rest it on the thigh for support. Rotate your left arm so the palm faces downward and reach it alongside the left ear and out to the right. Your whole being now is a straight line from your left outer foot to your left fingertips; make sure and keep the left outer foot and heel in strong contact with the floor.

Reverse on the other side (illustrated on opposite page).

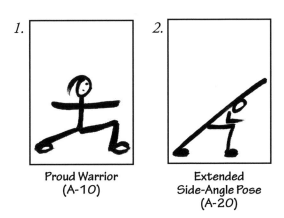

1. **Proud Warrior**
(A-10)

2. **Extended
Side-Angle Pose**
(A-20)

Breath & Meditation

Nine **Complete Yoga Breaths** in the position; repeat in the opposite direction. Focus on a point on your right beyond your left hand; reverse on other side.

Anecdote

In yoga, the warrior essence is in complete commitment to the task at hand, the purity of the line and the integrity of the whole.

Anatomy & Physiology

This asana calls on all the systems of the body for coordination and control, including the nervous system, sensory system and endocrine system.

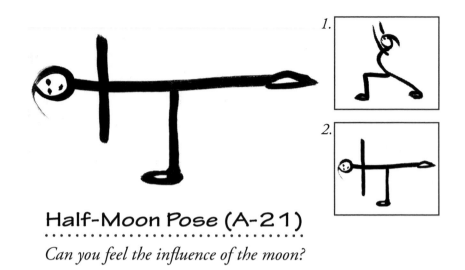

Half-Moon Pose (A-21)

Can you feel the influence of the moon?

Description

This asana engages the stabilizing core in new-found ways; perhaps creating new brain cells? It is precisely the same as **Warrior One** at inception, and moves into this grand variation of standing on one leg.

Instruction

Stand wide-legged, strong contact with floor through the feet, strong core, and spread your arms out to the sides. Turn your feet and hips and torso to face right, letting the ball of the left foot rotate inward to follow the move; bend the right knee and keep it stable over the right foot. The hands reach overhead.

Now, on to Half-Moon Pose (illustrated)!

Look forward, shift your weight onto the right foot, take a deep breath and come up over your right leg as you straighten it, bringing the left foot/leg off the floor and level with your torso. With both legs straight, standing on the right leg, keep lifting and drawing the left hip higher to flatten the levitating body. Alternate sides.

Breath & Meditation

Do the **Sounding Breath** and listen to the internal movement of your breath like the waves in the ocean.

Anecdote

In Sanskrit, *ha* means the sun - the creative force; *tha* means the moon – the receptive force. One is no good without the other. Hatha Yoga is the study of these two forces intrinsic in nature.

Anatomy & Physiology

This asana calls on all the systems of the body for balance, coordination and control, including the nervous system, sensory system, and endocrine system.

Side-Leg Lift (A-22)

Ever seen a dog or cat stretch out one leg at a time?

Description
This is an intensely stretching asana for the muscles in the legs.

Instruction
Stand with feet parallel, hip width apart. Lift the left leg and clasp the big toe between thumb and fingers (index and middle). Stretch the leg out to the side, straight as you can, and reach the right arm up and out. Reverse to other side.

Breath & Meditation
Select a spot or point on the wall or out the window directly in front of you.

Keep your eyes focused on this point – *drishti (gaze) point* in Sanskrit.

Anecdote
Some people think of focusing on one specific point as "navel gazing." Whatever point one chooses to focus on, it's considered to be the belly-button of the universe at that particular moment and place in time.

Anatomy & Physiology
This asana calls on all the systems of the body for coordination and control, including the nervous system, sensory system, and endocrine system.

Revolved Side-Angle Pose (A-23)

Why do we struggle to come to stillness?

Description

This asana is a wide open position demanding core strength, balance and coordination. It is precisely the same as ***Extended Side-Angle Pose*** in every aspect, except the variation in the revolved position of the extended torso and the arms. The back of the head is what you see in the illustration.

Instruction

Stand wide-legged, strong contact with floor through the feet, strong core, and spread your arms out to the sides. Turn your right foot so the toes face right. You can do this by simply lifting and rotating the ball of the foot and leaving the heel in place. Let the ball of the left foot likewise rotate inward to point in the same direction. Your hips are facing forward and your toes are facing right. Bend the right knee so the thigh eventually comes parallel to the floor with the knee directly over the right foot. The left leg stays straight and the left heel pushes outward to keep grounded. (see box #1)

Now onward to the Extended Side-Angle Pose:

Reach your right arm and your torso out over your bent knee. Bend the elbow and rest it on the thigh for support. Rotate your left arm so the palm faces downward and reach it alongside the left ear and out to the right. Your whole being now is a straight line from your left outer foot to your left fingertips; make sure and keep the left outer foot and heel in strong contact with the floor. (see box #2)

Now on to Revolved Side-Angle Pose (illustrated - box #3)

Bring that left arm across and down and press the back of the arm against the outside of the right leg. Reach that right arm upward so the palm faces behind you; your head and torso also face behind you.

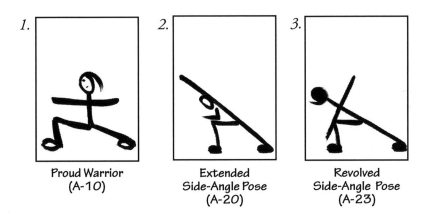

1. Proud Warrior
(A-10)

2. Extended
Side-Angle Pose
(A-20)

3. Revolved
Side-Angle Pose
(A-23)

Breath & Meditation

Use a big book or a one-foot block on the floor outside the right foot. Let the left hand brace and/or push against that block for support to help rotate the body. The physical wrestling with your own body here is the meditation. Observe how you deal with frustration; keep working through internal/mental blocks using your breath. Reverse on other side.

Anecdote

In yoga, the warrior essence is in the complete commitment to the task at hand.

Anatomy & Physiology

This asana calls on all the systems of the body for coordination and control, including the nervous system, sensory system, and endocrine system. It calls on all the energy of the mind and heart for patience and a sense of humor.

Revolved Triangle (A-24)

Is life full of twists and turns?
Have you ever experienced a complete rotation in your thinking?

Description

This asana takes you beyond what seems possible. It starts with **Triangle Pose** and moves into complete rotation of the torso. The back of the head is what you see in the illustration.

Instruction

Stand with feet wider apart than hips (standing wide-leg position). Open the arms wide, feeling the dynamic opposition in the chest and upper back. Keep the hips stable, facing forward, but rotate the balls of the feet to face right. Turn the right palm upward and reach out to the right as far as you can go, then drop the arm and rest the back of the hand along the inner right leg or down toward the ankle. The left arm simply reaches upward. Your two legs and your hips form a triangular shape. Open, reach, press and lengthen. The right side of your body, right arm, and right leg form another triangular shape. Imagine you are against a flat plane and bring your upper back and head and hips along that plane internally. (see box #1)

Now, on to the Revolved Triangle (illustrated - box #2)

Bring that left arm across and down and reach it toward the outside of the right leg; reach that right arm upward so the palm faces behind you; your head and torso also face behind you. To come out - breathe in and lift the arms to bring you upright. Reverse on the other side.

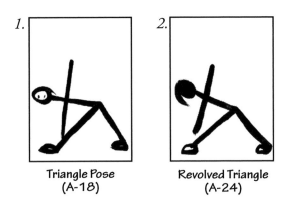

1. Triangle Pose
(A-18)

2. Revolved Triangle
(A-24)

Breath & Meditation

Use a big book or a one-foot block on the floor outside the right foot. Let the left hand brace and/or push against that block for support to help rotate the body. The physical wrestling with your own body here is the meditation. Observe how you deal with frustration; keep working through internal/mental blocks using your breath.

Anecdote

What, me worry? This is the wrestling of the spirit with the body.

Anatomy & Physiology

Wrings out and massages all the digestive organs.

Tortoise (A-25)

What is the average life-span of the Tortoise?

Description

This is an ancient Chinese deep-release for the brain.

Instruction

Sit or stand and hunch the shoulders up as high as you can, so they nestle the base of the skull and come up close to the ears. Keep the shoulders up, drawing them together toward the ears. Now, ever-so-gently, rock your skull in this self-made cradle. Hum while you rock and feel the vibration in the hum. Let your mouth be slightly open and let the rocking motion be slight. Try holding the ***Tortoise*** fifteen to thirty seconds or so, or more if you like. When you're ready to come out, lift the nose to bring the head back to a neutral position; then drop the head forward and give a sigh. Repeat once and hold a little longer. Never force this ancient practice. To get any benefit, it must be gently enjoyed.

Breath & Meditation

The ***Tortoise*** is a meditation on the base of the brain. Don't forget the humming as it adds so much to the experience.

Anecdote

This ancient practice, so they say, reverses the aging process.

Anatomy & Physiology

Releases tension in the shoulders, neck, throat, jaw, skull and upper back.

Eagle (A-26)

Can you observe your own thoughts like an eagle searching for prey?

Description

This asana requires the eagle's powerful concentration and strength.

Instruction

Stand with the feet hip-width apart and parallel. Stretch your arms out wide like wings. At the same time, lift the right leg and wrap it around the left; try and get the right foot stationary behind the left calf (it helps to draw the knee up high and across to start). Simultaneously wrap the right arm under the left in front of the chest. Bring the right fingertips to press against the left palm (palms are facing).

Breath & Meditation

Try the **Bastriki-Bellows** (also known as the **Breath of Fire**) - the light, panting, quick breath. Do thirty or more breaths. Stop and sit down if you get the least bit dizzy. As a further challenge, try to bow from the hips and bring the forehead to the knee.

Anecdote

In the yogic tradition, one who can sustain the **Eagle** for more than a minute and then bow into the **Sleeping Eagle** can overcome all obstacles.

Anatomy & Physiology

Said to be a preventive for prostate cancer; also a powerful strengthener for inner thighs, legs, ankles, feet, and abdominal core.

Arching Reach (A-27)

Why do we always seem to long upward rather than downward?

Description

This is nearly the same as the **Farmers Pose** but with an arm variation.

Instruction

Stand with the feet parallel, hip-width apart. Bring the hands behind with the elbows bent to press the palms against the lower back (sacrum area). Lift the head and look up as you press against the sacrum and lift the chest. Now release the hands and reach the arms straight overhead with palms facing (illustrated). Notice how the head may easily droop back. The knees may be straight this time; but it also works with them relaxed. Keep the chest yearning and reaching upward.

Breath & Meditation

Breathe in through the nasal passages; breathe out through the mouth or nose. Take twelve **Complete Yoga Breaths** if possible when you're arched up in the posture. The meditation here is in staying focused on the breath.

Anecdote

In the yogic tradition, desire is *rajas*, inertia is *tamas*. Lucidity - devoid of conceptual filters and emotional overlays, is called *sattva*.

Anatomy & Physiology

Massages and relaxes the muscles supporting the vertebrae of the spine.

Flat Back (A-28)

Can you describe your own back?

Description

This asana lengthens and strengthens the whole torso, creating one line from the base of the spine to the crown of the head.

Instruction

Stand in wide-leg position with feet parallel. Relax the knees. Engage your core abdominal muscles by drawing the navel and lower belly muscles in toward your back and sacrum. While holding the core muscles strong, hinge at the hip sockets (show hip sockets on skeletal poster and find a hinge action example in the room). When the torso is parallel to the floor, try and lengthen through your collarbone and neck; also bring the crown of your head in line with the whole spine. The arms can dangle or reach forward.

Breath & Meditation

Focus on ***Bastriki-Bellows Breath*** (also known as the ***Breath of Fire***) and keep it a light, panting breath. Try and breathe thirty to sixty rounds before you release and hang over. Relax the knees, engage your core strength, and slowly come back to standing upright.

Anecdote

It's said that when you gradually return to standing after ***Flat Back***, your head will seem to float and your mental state be euphoric.

Anatomy & Physiology

Strengthens muscle systems that support the spine; engages core strength and stretches and tones muscles that support the entire torso.

Standing Backbend (A-29)

What does an "open heart" mean?

Description

This asana is considered a heart opener and strengthener.

Instruction

Stand with the feet together and parallel. Engage all the muscles from the waist down; draw the glutes tight, legs straight, no bend in the knees, push down with the feet. This wrapping and tightening of all the muscles of the legs, thighs and buttocks creates a strong base (like a stiff vase) for your ***Standing Backbend***. Keeping this base strong, bring your hands behind to press against your lower back; look up, reach your arms up, and go into your backbend. The action here is in strongly lifting the breastbone (sternum) while the arms are reaching. The more energy you bring to lifting the breastbone directly upward, the deeper the experience of the ***Backbend***.

Breath & Meditation

Focus on breathing from the area of your chest where the heart is. Try nine full breaths if possible in this position.

Anecdote

This posture lifts the spirits as it lifts the heart.

Anatomy & Physiology

Backward bends in yoga are said to open the heart. They stretch and tone the muscles between the ribs, along with the deep core muscles of the whole torso. They stimulate circulation and bring more energy to the lungs and heart.

Shiva's Pose (A-30)

What do you think "no creation without destruction" means?

Description

This asana is a metaphor for destroying the old mindset and beginning anew.

Instruction

Stand with feet turned out at a 45-degree angle (duck footed). Put all the weight on the right foot and lift the left foot high, turned out, heel flexed, with the left knee raised above the hips. Let the right knee bend, also turned out, in line over the right foot. Bring the right arm overhead and reach down behind your back. Bring the left arm under around back and reach up. Clasp hands as close as possible behind your back. When the raised foot comes crashing down, one world is destroyed and another begins. Reverse sides.

Breath & Meditation

Focus on breathing in and out from the "third eye." Try and stay nine breaths in the posture.

Anecdote

This asana represents consciously letting go of the old, negative patterns so fresh energy can come in.

Anatomy & Physiology

This posture stretches the upper arms and shoulders, while calling on left-brain, right-brain coordination to stand on one foot with the other leg lifted.

Everyday Yoga Lessons on the Mat - B

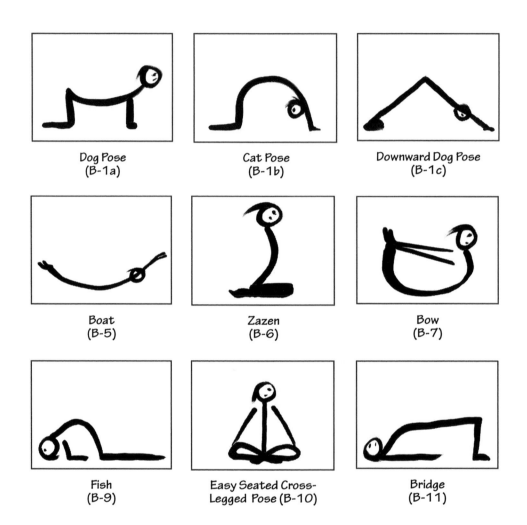

Dog Pose
(B-1a)

Cat Pose
(B-1b)

Downward Dog Pose
(B-1c)

Boat
(B-5)

Zazen
(B-6)

Bow
(B-7)

Fish
(B-9)

Easy Seated Cross-
Legged Pose (B-10)

Bridge
(B-11)

Everyday Yoga Lessons on the Mat - B

Upward Dog Pose
(B-2)

Child's Pose
(B-3)

Cobra
(B-4)

Shoulder Stand
(B-8a)

Plow
(B-8b)

Wind-Relieving Pose
(B-8c)

Float
(B-12)

Everyday Yoga Lessons - B
are postures where floor contact is required;
so here you will need yoga mats.

Dog / Cat / Downward Dog (B-1)

Come to the floor on hands and knees, like a **Dog** or a **Cat** in four-legged position. Let the back extend, as if you are reaching up and behind with your tailbone (coccyx), and the head and chest lift. Breathe in. This is called the **Dog Pose**. Hands are a bit further forward than the shoulder sockets and knees are under the hip sockets and hip-width apart.

1.

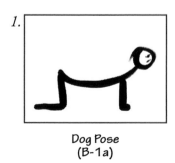

Dog Pose
(B-1a)

Roll your toes under. Roll or tuck your tailbone and head under. Engage your abdominal muscles by drawing your belly and ribs upward toward your spine. Round your spine and draw it upward toward the ceiling. This is called the **Cat Pose** . In the **Cat Pose** you exhale and draw your abdominal muscles inward on the exhale, which feels quite natural and accentuates the pose.

2.

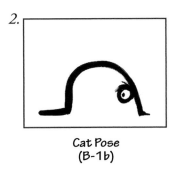

Cat Pose
(B-1b)

Shift back into **Dog** , breathe in, press the hands and toes into the floor and lift the hips with the sitting bones reaching up and back. (Use anatomy poster for clarity – where exactly are the sitting bones?)

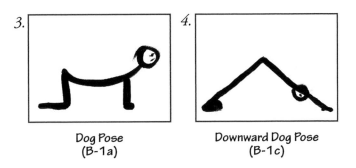

3. Dog Pose
(B-1a)

4. Downward Dog Pose
(B-1c)

You want your spine straight and long, so relax the knees slightly, then try straightening the legs and stretching the heels toward the floor. This is called the **Downward Dog Pose**. Chances are you've seen dogs stretch like this. The shoulder blades roll luxuriantly skyward toward the hips; the entire torso frame is long and straightens more and more (with luck).

Notice how engaging the abdominal muscles helps you lift into the **Downward Dog** and keep it strong.

The trick is not to push down into the hands but to lift up your behind. All the fingers are spread apart; try and use the strength in the first digits of the fingers, nearest the palms.

Upward Dog (B-2)

Without further ado, roll down and come through into *Upward Dog*.

or:

Drop the knees. Shift the hips all the way back and down to the heels. You may stay here resting if you like and call this *Child's Pose*.

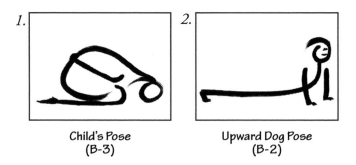

1. Child's Pose
(B-3)

2. Upward Dog Pose
(B-2)

Look forward and draw the chest toward the floor. Your elbows are deeply bent. Press on the hands and scroll forward and through at the same time straightening the legs, making them strong by reaching back with the heels and lifting the backs of the knees up. This is the *Upward Dog*. Here it's pictured with the toes rolled under. It may also be done with the tops of the feet on the floor.

Try to not slump in the middle but engage and draw in the core muscles and keep breathing.

Child's Pose (B-3)

When you drop back from being on your hands and knees, or from **Upward Dog (B-2)**, let your hips sink back onto your heels and let your forehead rest on the floor. This is a good posture for deeply releasing any tension in the lower back. You may fold your arms and clasp your hands behind your back (illustrated), rest them at your sides, or stretch them forward into an extended **Child's Pose**. It's good to stay here a minute or so, especially if your lower back needs a rest. The toes are closer together here than the heels, and the soles of the feet face upward.

Cobra (B-4)

All you need to do here is pretend you're coming out of your skin. Leave the old skin behind on the floor and let the heart and the mind pull you ahead. Start prone with chin resting on the floor and bring hands to the sides so the fingertips are even with the tops of the shoulders. Lift the head and look forward; uncurl the chest and head up slowly; pull with the hands and curve your chest up higher and higher. Shoulders draw down away from the ears and keep wide. Elbows stay drawn into the sides of your body and also bent (if need be) in order to bring the shoulders down and back from the ears. The hands on the floor at shoulder level are further apart than are the elbows. The big toes are close together, the heels drop outward, the legs are entirely on the floor, right along behind the grounded pelvis.

Boat (B-5)

Start prone with chin resting on the floor. Reach both arms forward alongside the head. Breathe in and draw straight arms and straight legs inches off the floor. Keep the neck relaxed and look out forward, but not up. Tighten the buttocks and take three or six breaths.

Zazen (B-6)

You'll recognize this pose as the sitting meditation posture from Japan. Soften your calve muscles, stretch out your ankles, and let the toes turn in toward each other and the heels open to the sides. Do not force this position. Use a pillow between your hips and your legs, if need be, to make it easier.

Bow (B-7)

Start prone with the chin resting on the floor. Bend the knees and reach around and clasp the feet with the hands. Take a deep breath and kick/push your feet against your hands, lifting the head and chest at the same time and looking forward. This will bring you into a bowed position. Rock forward and back. Breathe. Come down after three breaths.

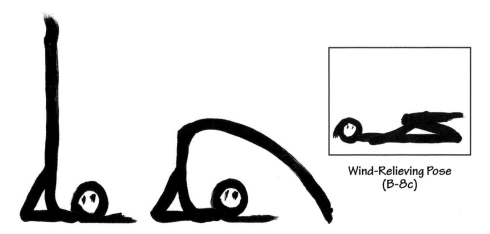

Wind-Relieving Pose
(B-8c)

Shoulder Stand, Plow & Wind-Relieving Pose (B-8)

Lie on your back in supine position. Roll your legs up over your head and support your back with your hands. Straighten the legs to the ceiling. The weight will be on your shoulders. If the weight is too much on the neck, then drop back down so the weight is on the shoulders. Breathe and take time to see how all this feels. Slowly let the legs begin to glide overhead behind you so eventually, perhaps, the toes rest on the floor. Do not force the feet to the floor. Come out gradually, with the legs straight, and rest by relaxing with the knees hanging over the chest. Gather the knees closer into the chest with the arms, hands clasped. We call this rest position the **Wind-Relieving Pose**. It soothes and relaxes all the muscles of the lower back, which have just been so deeply stretched.

Fish (B-9)

Lie on your back in supine position. Draw your elbows close into your sides. Push on the elbows and forearms and arch the chest. Let the head roll back to rest lightly on the floor. Make whatever adjustment you need to get comfortable and draw the chest even higher. The legs and feet are at ease. You've created a half-circle from your coccyx to the top of your head.

Easy Seated Cross-Legged Pose (B-10)

Sit cross-legged on the floor (illustrated). Let the head hang forward and drop the torso forward between your thighs, with your hands resting on the floor. You may try rocking and even humming as you rock side-to-side.

Bridge (B-11)

Lie on your back and draw your feet up under your knees. Keep your chin dropping and your neck relaxed as you push down with your feet (not only on the outer edge and not only on the inner edge; using the entire ball of the foot and especially the heel) and press your hips up. You may support your back with your hands (optional), clasp the hands along the floor (optional), or simply lengthen the arms along the floor (illustrated). Roll down slowly vertebrae by vertebrae. This posture works beautifully if you breathe in as you go up, and breathe out as you come slowly down.

Float (B-12)

In this position the body is totally at rest. It's an excellent position for eliciting the "relaxation response." The palms are turned upward with the arms at the sides. The chin is slightly down, which relaxes the area at the top of the neck in back, near the base of the skull. If a student feels any discomfort while lying on her back in this pose, have her turn over and lie face down, or on her side.

Partner Everyday Yoga Lessons - P

Assisted Stick (P-1)

Suspended Bridge / Suspended Squat (P-2)

Assisted Backbend (P-3)

Assisted Reach
(P-4)

Assisted
Slump / Hunch (P-5)

Assisted Breath
(P-6)

Assisted Stick (P-1)

Come into the **Standing Stick (A-9)** and have your partner support your outreached hands. (When working in threes, have one person support the hands or arms and the second person support the lifted leg.) Go for the straight stick, with both hip sockets the same distance from the floor and smooth, even, dynamic opposition. The supporting partners interfere as little as possible, observe closely, and go with the alignment and breathing rhythm of the acting partner. Then gradually, intuitively, help the acting partner to lengthen, stabilize and breathe evenly.

Suspended Bridge / Suspended Squat (P-2)

Face your partner and clasp each other's wrists firmly. Each party needs to hold on tight. Step backward, relax the knees, begin to hinge at the hips and draw/hang away from each other until you come to **Flat Back (A-28)** with relaxed, slightly bent knees. Your feet will be about three or four feet from your partner's feet.

You might also take this down into a **Suspended Squat**. Make sure you press your thighs out over the feet in the **Suspended Squat** (don't let your knees collapse inward towards each other - press them apart). The pleasure is in hanging away from each other and counter-balancing your weight.

Finally, in both these suspended positions, experience the awesome yielding and letting go all down through the lower back as well as the upper back, shoulders and neck.

Assisted Backbend (P-3)

Face your partner and clasp each other's wrists firmly. Each party needs to hold on tight. Have one partner support the other in a Standing Partial Backbend. This is a backbend with the arms reaching forward. (Not the **Standing Backbend (A-29)** where the arms are overhead.) The supporting partner relaxes the knees, sinks her weight back, and engages the core strength in order to do the supporting. The acting partner will probably go about a third of the way back toward the floor. Support the acting partner totally as he or she comes back up, then switch and have the other partner do the supporting.

Next, both parties can hang back simultaneously. Again, the plot is in pulling gently, softly, evenly away from each other and counter-balancing each other's weight.

Assisted Reach (P - 4)

Stand tall above and behind your acting partner. This may be done with the acting partner sitting on his own heels in *Zazen* or in *Easy Seated Cross-Legged Position* on the floor.

Have the acting (seated) partner reach up and clasp your wrists and assist him in reaching his arms higher while relaxing his shoulders - reaching with the upper back and chest as well as the arms. Suggest your partner drop or sink his base (tailbone) as he lifts his upper body and arms to experience dynamic opposition.

Switch positions.

Assisted Hunch/Slump (P- 5)

Stand behind your partner, reach around the waist and support him or her loosely, just below the rib cage. Bring your hands to clasp gently in front below the breastbone, just beneath and below the rib cage. Simply give support with your arms and breathe along together as he or she relaxes forward into the *Hunch/Slump (A-2)*.

Assisted Breath (P-6)

Observe your partner's breathing by watching closely and from different perspectives. Are they bringing the breath in fully so the belly and rib cage (diaphragm area) and upper chest expand on the inhale? Are they breathing out completely, or are they cutting short the exhale? If they don't exhale fully, they'll hold in stale air, starving them of oxygen. The lungs can't take in the new breath fully if they are not completely emptied of the old breath. Observe your partner's breathing from the back. Are the ribs in the upper back moving with the breath?

Now, give verbal feedback about how they might breathe more fully. Spread out your hands, thumbs touching across their upper back, rest them along the rib cage in back; encourage them to breathe so you feel their ribs expand on the inhale and release on the exhale.

Are they breathing mainly by only lifting their shoulders? Encourage them to relax their shoulders, and let the shoulder blades drop.

Is the jaw tight? The forehead? The knees? Encourage them to let go of any unnecessary tension by focusing on the long exhale.

Vinyasa / Flow Series - V

Vinyasa is Sanskrit for a flowing form of yoga in which postures are strung together like strings of beads. A slow or fast rhythm is created through the movement of the body in sync with the movement of the breath. As you will begin to feel and understand through yoga practice - any and all the postures may be connected and made into a "vinyasa" sequence.

Salutation to the Sun (V-1)

Salutation to the Moon (V-2)

Warrior Vinyasa (V-3)

One-Leg Vinyasa (V-4)

Salutation to the Sun (V-1)

Exhale

1. Mountain Pose
(A-6)

Inhale

2. Hanuman's Reach
(A-1)

Exhale

3. Forward Bend
(A-15)

Inhale

4. Hanuman's Lunge
(A-19)

Exhale

5. Downward Dog
(B-1)

Inhale

6. Upward Dog
(B-2)

Exhale

7. Downward Dog
(B-1)

Inhale

8. Hanuman's Lunge
(A-19)

Exhale

9. Forward Bend
(A-15)

Inhale

10. Hanuman's Reach
(A-1)

Exhale

11. Mountain Pose
(A-6)

*repeat
vinyasa
with
other leg
back*

Salutation to the Moon (V-2)

Exhale

1. Wide-Leg Mountain Pose (A-6)

Inhale

2. Wide-Leg Hanuman's Reach (A-1)

Exhale

3. Wide-Leg Forward Bend (A-7)

Inhale

4. *and hold on the turn*

Exhale

5. *on the upward reach, bend left knee*

Warrior One (A-17)

Inhale

6. *straighten left leg*

Exhale

7. *reach out over leg with arms and torso, round over, try to bring head to knee*

Standing Head-to-Knee Pose (V-a)

Inhale

8. *clasp hands behind the back*

Exhale

9. *the knee bends again and the torso moves inside the left leg to the grass.*

Snake to the Grass (V-b)

Inhale

10.

Exhale

11. Wide-Leg Mountain Pose (A-6)

Warrior Vinyasa (V-3)

1.

Mountain Pose
(A-6)

2.

Warrior One
(A-17)

3.

Proud Warrior
(A-10)

4.

Extended
Side-Angle Pose
(A-20)

5.

Proud Warrior
(A-10)

6.

Mountain Pose
(A-6)

Coordinate the breath.

*Try two or even three breaths
with each asana.*

One Leg Vinyasa (V-4)

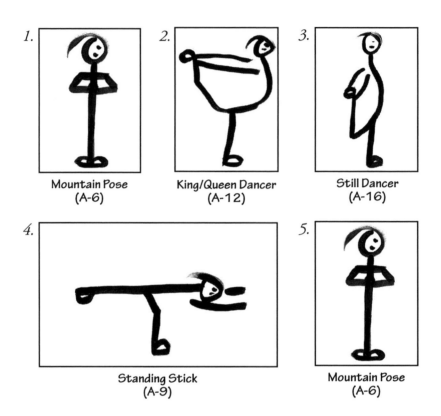

1. Mountain Pose
(A-6)

2. King/Queen Dancer
(A-12)

3. Still Dancer
(A-16)

4. Standing Stick
(A-9)

5. Mountain Pose
(A-6)

*Try doing this or some similar self-styled vinyasa sequence with a continuous **Bastriki-Bellows Breath** (also known as **Breath of Fire**) or **Sounding Breath**.*

Special Occasion Yoga Lessons

Yoga is the mother of stress management practices: it has been around for three thousand years and has given us techniques that help us acknowledge our self-doubts and insecurities, and yet be strong and do what's necessary.

"Yoga" actually means "*union*" in Sanskrit. Union of the different influences conflicting within us; integration of the will and desire with physical reality and actual possibility; union of each of us with all of us through awareness of how much we are alike in dreaming, hoping, fearing, and most of all, in our dependence on breath.

The practice of yoga gives us courage – the courage to be less than perfect, to fumble, to sometimes be clumsy, to take the risk of failing, and then to try again. To stay with the practice – watching ourselves do well on occasion and not so well on other occasions, teaches us emotional stamina, self-forgiveness, compassion for ourselves and others.

Even the most conscientious, hard-working individuals sometimes go into states of anxious denial or dismissive states of passivity before exams and tests.

Stretching, focusing on a mantra, or an image, or the breath, gives us a much-needed moment to ponder. As the nervous system calms – a result, apparently, of self-acceptance, our breath keeps speaking to us, whispering to us, "I'm in control here. I can do this. I'll do my best and it's okay to be nervous."

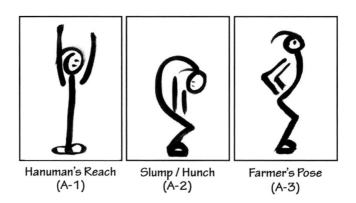

Hanuman's Reach
(A-1)

Slump / Hunch
(A-2)

Farmer's Pose
(A-3)

Exams and Tests

- Create a three-to-six-minute "stress-relief practice" for the whole class to do before an exam. For example, *Hanuman's Pose (A-1)* through *Farmer's Pose (A-3)* for two or three rounds may be easily done seated or standing.

- Create a six-minute "vigorous stress-relief practice" using *Hanuman's Pose (A-1)*, *Slump/Hunch (A-2)*, *Farmer's Pose (A-3)* and *Standing Stick (A-9)* for at least two rounds, along with the *Breath of Fire*. Adding the intense *Stick Pose* creates a demanding challenge.

- Using the verbal instructions for each asana/breath/meditation, have one student at a time lead so that you, the teacher, may listen, give up directing things, and do the sequence with your students before the exam.

- Help each student create a three-to-six-minute "personal stress-relief practice." Have them report to you either verbally or in writing what their practice consists of, and how well it did or did not work for them. Help them keep refining these sequences until they are effective in relieving stress.

- Have the students in groups create a "stress-relief practice" for the whole class to do before an exam. Try the different practices – postures, breathing techniques and meditations, and let the class decide what works best for them. Encourage students to take turns leading the practice before an exam.

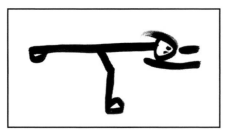

Standing Stick (A-9)

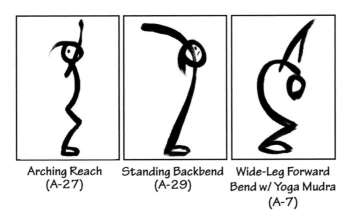

Arching Reach
(A-27)

Standing Backbend
(A-29)

Wide-Leg Forward
Bend w/ Yoga Mudra
(A-7)

Presentations and Oral Reports

- Create a sequence or a single asana/breath/meditation practice that everyone does alone before they present or speak in front of the classroom – i.e., *Arching Reach (A-27)*, *Standing Backbend (A-29)*, and *Wide-Leg Forward Bend with Yoga Mudra (A-7)*.

- Write a sequence of postures and breaths on a card and hand it out to the presenting student a day or so beforehand. Give the student space and time to practice the sequence immediately before they present in school.

- Encourage the students to evaluate whether or not the practice helped them with their self-confidence and overall presentation. Have students give you feedback on their findings.

First Day of School, Last Day of School, Special Assembly

- Point out how Hatha Yoga is an exploration. Explorers, as we all know, take many wrong paths and may become disillusioned; but they transcend these feelings and rise above them to gain new ground.

- Explore several postures with your students in an open exchange.

- Have your students lead other classes or the entire school population in a sequence that builds up to one of the *Vinyasa Series – Salutation to the Sun or Moon*. Encourage everyone to follow along as best they can and to observe for themselves how they handle frustration, self-consciousness, bashfulness, the desire to be perfect, boredom, weariness, self-loathing, and embarrassment. These are emotions and self-judgments that we all have sometimes.

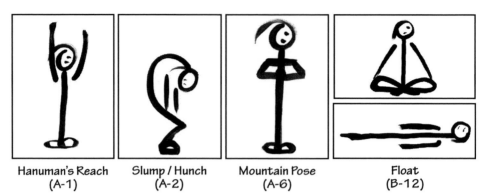

Hanuman's Reach (A-1)   Slump / Hunch (A-2)   Mountain Pose (A-6)   Float (B-12)

Any Occasion When You Feel Under Stress

- Fifteen-second quick-relief technique:

    one **Complete Yoga Breath** deeply felt in belly, rib cage, and upper chest.

- Thirty-second quick-relief technique:

    three **Complete Yoga Breaths** deeply felt in belly, rib cage, and upper chest.

- Mantra:

    either your own or the traditional *om*, which means peace, spoken silently along
    with the exhale.

    > *or*

    either your own or the traditional *om*, which means peace, repeated over
    and over silently along with a series of inhales and exhales.

- One school made up its own three-part mantra, done with three postures:

    Yoga wakes me up – **Hanuman's Pose (A-1)**
    Yoga calms me down – **Slump/Hunch (A-2)**
    Yoga lets me be – **Mountain Pose (A-6)**

- Twenty-minute deep relaxation:

    lying down in **Float / Corpse (B-12)** pose,

    > *or*

    sitting in a comfortable position with the head on the desk,

    > *or*

    sitting in **Zazen**, or **Easy Seated Cross-Legged Pose**, perhaps on a pillow, and:
    - repeating the mantra and detaching from passing thoughts and feelings.

        > *or*

    - observing the breath and detaching from passing thoughts and feelings.

        > *or*

    - focusing on a tiny light in the center of the consciousness, the "third eye,"
      and detaching from passing thoughts and feelings.

Individual Therapeutic Applications

Yoga is a holistic practice. Postures, breathing techniques and meditative techniques are beneficial for everyone. If we are hyper, they calm us down; if we are lethargic, they get us energized. Since the entire practice is based on self-awareness, breath, gentle persistence, and self-exploration, there is no forcing, no hurry, and no failure!

Therapeutic Yoga Teaching Practices

- Try to set aside critical judgment. Each time you feel the need to correct and judge, do the **Complete Yoga Breath** – so you (the teacher) feel centered and grounded. Say "Oh well," with each exhalation and watch the need pass.

- Encourage students to pretty much create their own practice from the simple tools you give them. Self-empowerment leads to self-regulation.

- Allow students to discover the benefits of the practice for themselves. Do not set up goals in their minds or expectations.

- Look for ways to have students express what's happening in their yoga experience; i.e., open class discussion, journaling, leading other classmates, revolving leadership, writing an essay about the experience, singing, drawing, painting, sculpting or staging a play.

- Take the time to help individual students settle on two or three techniques they may use throughout the school day for their specific needs; i.e., before an exam, the beginning of the day, every time they feel threatened or anxious. Students may do a technique silently, when under stress, and no one else needs to know they are doing it.

Attention deficit disorder, insomnia, anxiety, depression, aggressive or violent behavior, bipolar disorder, anorexia, bulimia, hyperactivity, dyslexia, obsessive-compulsive – almost any disorder you find among young people today may be helped by yoga practice. Often, those with "syndromes" and "disorders" are full of creative energy. Yoga is a non-threatening, non-invasive means of channeling this energy into self-awareness, self-acceptance and mental clarity.

As teachers your intent is simply to have the student take the time to breathe and look inward. This slows and concentrates the thought process and focuses the mind. Combining the breathing and mindfulness with a variety of stretches and postures sets an awakening process in motion that is deeply healing and balancing.

I. Hyperactivity / Attention Deficit & Bipolar Disorder

Teach your students *Everyday Yoga Lessons Standing A-1 through A-8*, paying particular attention to the breathing. Read over the lessons first and think about the questions, descriptions, instructions, breaths/meditations and anecdotes as they are presented in each lesson. This *A-1* through *A-8* series takes the student from energizing and grounding experiences to deep release and balancing experiences, leading to greater concentration, confidence, and right brain / left brain coordination. Have students repeat the series in the classroom on a regular basis. Help them explore and present (or not) what they are experiencing. They may draw sketches or write down how they feel after each practice session, or they may show you or tell you.

Keep in mind that in this process, students are becoming more and more aware of what sets them off – where they loose touch with themselves. This self-knowledge, which they are gaining, is reinforced in a natural way by continued practice and by learning new postures.

II. Depression / Insomnia / Anxiety

Start by observing the student's breath while breathing along with him or her and doing the *Complete Yoga Breath* together. The object is to increase the oxygen to the brain, which gives one an immediate sensation of feeling better. Do the *Bastriki Breath* (also known as *Breath of Fire*) with them for five seconds, fifteen seconds, up to thirty seconds. Get feedback.

Introduce them to the twelve postures in *Everyday Lessons B* and (if possible) do the postures with them.

Teach them the *Sounding Breath* as a three to five-minute meditation with them sitting with their heads on the desks, in *Zazen*, *Easy Seated Cross-Legged Pose* or lying on the floor in *Float Pose*.

Move on to finding ways to get them involved in observing their own breath throughout the day, i.e., with a few minutes practice of postures and breathing each morning.

Get written or oral feedback often.

Chances are by now the energy level is up, oxygen uptake has dramatically improved, and students will be more receptive to immersing themselves in yoga practice in a myriad of ways. By all means encourage them to do so!

III. Anorexia / Bulimia

Start with breathing together in postures *A-1, A-2, A-3, A-7, A-8, A-10*.

In *A-1*, use phrases like "Fill on the inhale, hold it, take in more." In *A-2*, use phrases like "Empty completely on the exhale, let it all go, let the exhale be longer than the inhale." These suggestions give the student the experience of a satisfying, self-nurturing fullness on the one hand, and the experience of total cleansing emptiness on the other hand.

Keep this focus on breathing and move ahead through the series at your (the teacher's) pace. *Wide-Leg Forward Bend with Yoga Mudra (A-7)* opens the heart, *Standing Knee-to-Chest (A-8)* is a balancing pose that instills confidence, *Proud Warrior (A-10)* is a self-empowering pose, where the student stands bravely breathing in a fresh internal environment.

Yoga is known as a purification process: You draw in fresh insight and wisdom on the inhale and let go everything you don't need on the exhale. The sense of personal power and self-acceptance are enhanced by this conscious breathing.

Follow the asana practice with *Progressive Muscle Relaxation* – with the head on the desk or lying in *Float Pose (B-12)* on the floor. End the session with *A Peaceful Place Visualization*.

After the first or second session, impress on the student how yoga places a high value on each individual's internal experience. How we appear to others is arbitrary, we have no control of it; it's impossible for us to know and manipulate how others see us and what they think of us. What's important is our own experience of being alive. And no one can take that away from us.

Suggest that students keep a journal about their yoga experience. Emphasize how the journal is private – it belongs only to the student (unless they volunteer to share it).

IV. Aggressiveness / Anger & Violent / Disruptive Behavior

Young people with lots of resentment and anger, who tend to act out and become violent, respond to the internal order and security and reassurance of yoga practice. Respect for each individual's private experience; space and time to pay close attention to what one feels – these are the simple tools that often bring about felicitous change.

Remember, the teacher/facilitator does not pry into those feelings, but simply encourages students to acknowledge them to themselves – no matter what they are. All feelings are equal in yoga, when we observe them with detachment. The practice gives students concrete tools and resources for self-control and self-regulation. It gives them power over themselves, where before they felt powerless.

Show them the illustrations and ask them to try doing *Everyday Lessons A-1 through A-10*. This series challenges the body and disciplines the mind. Students become more mentally alert and attentive, as they are called upon to use all their capacities at once. The series also educates the student in concepts like "grounding," "centering," "core strength," "concentration," "balance," "focus," and "open-mindedness."

Once students are receptive, teach them to extend the exhale in the Complete Yoga Breath while doing the posture, and/or try a short suspension of the breath at the end of the exhale before the next inhale. This gives the student the ability to overcome the knee-jerk response by pausing before reacting.

Give students an assignment to work on the more difficult postures like *Eagle (A-26)*, and *Shiva's Pose (A-30)*. Think of ways and means for them to express what they are experiencing and communicate it to family members, classmates, and teachers.

Lead your students through the *Third Eye Visualization/Meditation* with them sitting in *Zazen* or *Easy Seated Cross-Legged Pose*, or lying down in *Float Pose*.

V. Dyslexia & Obsessive-Compulsive Disorder

It's important to look over the descriptions carefully and slowly with the student or students. Start with *A-1* and *A-2*, and have students study the illustrations and imitate the postures. These two postures are simple, but the important thing for the new yoga student is to consciously breathe and become aware of how it feels to stretch up as high as you can, then release and let go. This process only happens over time with repetition. Your role is NOT to correct but simply to witness and encourage. That is what's challenging for school teachers. So often, they want to jump in and have students get it right! Resist the urge. The only "right" here is to become more and more aware of the breath. Make it clear that there's no way the student can get it wrong, since it's just an exploration.

Have students draw stick figures or make clay models for *Everyday Lessons A-1 through A-8*, and suggest they begin to do their routine on a regular basis, either at home or in school. Have them do the sequence for you, with you, for the class or leading the class.

Yoga trains the mind to be attentive and nothing is irrelevant. Images, imaginings, sounds, memories, emotions, impulses - all of these are grist for the mill (as they say), but in yoga one learns to turn the focus back to the breath. All these influences come and go, while the breath remains.

namaste

Bibliography

Relax & Renew: Restful Yoga for Stressful Times, by Judith Lasater

The Shambhala Encyclopedia of Yoga, by Georg Feuerstein

Moving Into Stillness, by Erich Schiffman

The Heart of Yoga, by T.K.V. Desikachar

The Sivananda Companion to Yoga, by Sivananda Yoga Center

The Art of Yoga, by BKS Iyengar

The Wheels of Life, by Anodea Judith

Autobiography of a Yogi, by P. Yogananda

Living With the Himalayan Masters, by Swami Rama

Surya Namaskara, by Swami Satyananda Saraswati

Beyond the Relaxation Response, by Dr. H. Benson

Treat Your Own Back, by Robin Mckenzie

About Us

· · · · · · · · · · · · ·

At **Yoga Mountain,** we speak of yoga as the art of gentle persistence, because this is what experience has taught us. Strength comes in relaxation and yielding; mastery comes in grace and effortlessness. We encourage students to attend yoga classes designed for all levels, as we are all beginners at heart and learn best in this open, generous environment. Advanced students are challenged to go deeper into the postures.

Yoga Mountain draws on a variety of asana and pranayama styles and traditions, both ancient and modern, and combines them into an integrated practice of Hatha Yoga and mindful meditation. To break down resistance to change, one may sometimes need dynamic, flowing vinyasa sequences; at other times reality may be such that one needs gentle, healing, restorative work. Gail Walsh describes the *Yoga Mountain* approach as a journey of growing awareness in both these aspects of reality: *"ha"* – the sun – the surging, creative force, and *"tha"* – the moon – the receptive, grounding force. In Sanskrit, the word *"Hatha"* means **sun** and **moon**, the word *"yoga"* means **union.**

Website: **www.yogamountain.com**
Contact the author: **gailwalsh@yogamountain.com**

Classroom Notes

Classroom Notes
· · · · · · · · · · · · · · · · · ·

Classroom Notes

Classroom Notes

Classroom Notes

Classroom Notes